LOVE MINUS LOVE

Wayne Holloway-Smith was born in Wiltshire and lives in London. His first book-length collection *Alarum* (Bloodaxe Books, 2017), was a Poetry Book Society Wild Card Choice for Winter 2017, was shortlisted for the Roehampton Poetry Prize 2017 and for the Seamus Heaney Centre for Poetry Prize for First Full Collection 2018, and longlisted for the 2019 Michael Murphy Memorial Prize for a distinctive first book of poetry. The final poem in the collection, 'Short', won the Geoffrey Dearmer Prize 2016. His box of poetry, *I CAN'T WAIT FOR THE WENDING*, was published by Test Centre Publications in 2018. He won the National Poetry Competition 2018 for 'the posh mums are boxing in the square' from his second collection, *Love Minus Love* (Bloodaxe Books, 2020), also a Poetry Book Society Wild Card Choice.

WAYNE HOLLOWAY-SMITH

LOVE MINUS LOVE

BLOODAXE BOOKS

ISBN: 978 1 78037 508 3

First published 2020 by
Bloodaxe Books Ltd
Eastburn
South Park
Hexham
Northumberland NE46 1BS

www.bloodaxebooks.com
For further information about Bloodaxe titles
please visit our website and join our mailing list
or write to the above address for a catalogue.

Supported using public funding by
ARTS COUNCIL
ENGLAND

Printed in Great Britain by Bell & Bain Limited, Glasgow, Scotland, on
acid-free paper sourced from mills with FSC chain of custody certification.

for my mother, for her courage

for Sarah and Margot, for being the best

ACKNOWLEDGEMENTS

Thanks to the editors of the following publications in which some extracts of this book appeared: *Bath Magg*, *The Believer*, *Poetry*, *Poetry London*, *The Poetry Review*, *The Rialto*, *The Scores*. Some moments from the text also appeared in *I CAN'T WAIT FOR THE WENDING* (Test Centre, 2018). Pages 56/57, beginning 'the posh mums are boxing in the square', won the National Poetry Competition 2018.

A massive thanks to Heather Phillipson, Jack Underwood, Jess Chandler, Mark Waldron, Emily Berry, Nuar Alsadir, Jericho Brown, Helen Charman, Raymond Antrobus, Anthony Anaxagorou and Sandeep Parmar for their invaluable support, advice, friendship. Thanks also to Arts Council England for the Project Grant, and to Liverpool John Moores University for the Fellowship, both of which provided me with the time and space to produce this book.

CONTENTS

Love Minus Love *9*

NOTES *63*

Icouldbeafreegratefulguilt
beanuntroubleduntyrannic
erbuttothisendeverythingth
onethatisweourselvesshoul

lessuprightsonandyoucould
alsympatheticcontentedfath
ateverhappenedwouldbeund
dhavecancelledeachotherout

I can tell you the first person I wanted to look like was
      Bonnie Langford
the second was the deciduous tree
just far enough from my childhood home
I could see it if I walked out
and slammed the door shut forever
      you keep the leaves that tree has thrown off David
and I'll be its body of twigs

elsewhere I'm standing with my hands

in my jacket pockets

and watching a young boy step off his bike

and step into a shop with its light and daytime booze

and watching with my hands in my jacket pockets a grown adult

man step out of that shop

a roll-up hung outside of itself and off his lower lip step

onto that kid's bike my hands are in my pockets I'm watching

him ride it half-way down the road now he is stepping off it

like it's nothing with my hands in my pockets

I'm watching him like it's nothing no bad thing no guilt

throw it break it against the ground I am praying hands

in my pockets

right there that that bike will rise from its shallow grave

at the edge of a main road

in a very physical sense sheer machinery-like

praying for that kid's bike to follow

and keep that grown man forever   like the knowledge

I keep that everything is my fault and is there waiting outside

all the cake shops the swimming pools with their chlorine the butchers

meanwhile the woman who will one day be your mother
is busy turning her belly into a butcher's shop
busy making her bed and laying in it
shaming says her family *its business*
with what is suddenly inside her body's display windows

when for the full term she has stood behind its counter
she'll palm two halves of a baby cow to someone
with rolled up sleeves the first will be taken
and buried in the ground
the other she will wrench back
and for hours with weeping hold
gift-wrapped in kraft paper

what
is
the
least
a
person
can
reduce
themselves
to
maybe
I'm sorry
or

hi
these
two
things
take
the
consumption
of
verylittlemeat
to
achieve
verylittleeggyolk
to
maintain
no milk

hi   your mum is explaining
to you about menstrual cycles
blood – an unflushed bowl   your mum is following you
room to room teaching you how to hoover *one day*
she says *your wife will thank me*
your mum is standing looking very tall   your mum drunk
you say hard things out loud even when they hurt
your mum smoking and eating chocolate
crying in the kitchen   on Sundays

keep the photo of my dad smoking and looking like James Dean

I've been so lovingly breathed into by the empty promise

of that cigarette   that kiss-curled head in that black and white photo   he is
   my age

or younger he is maybe fifteen   in that photo back knuckled to his own dad's
   barn door

he is slender in too-tight jeans he is going to do something

shallow soon and very bad

                 I'm trying hard to follow his example but I don't want to die

I can't seem to lift a heavy thing or get into fights pass the lighter

I just like smoking   and watching TV

silent like his photo in his eulogy they said he loved beef always beef in his
   sandwiches

his hair is receding he is being very attractive   in his photo he is going to do
   something

very soon he is gone it's already done

here's your mother she is sleeping
dressed in ostentatious pink
in the passenger seat of a brown–beige Vauxhall Cavalier
   her hair done perfect curated   the windows done
up tight the exhaust fumes are your father gently filling up the car

[I wish I could tell you openly of the things that went on in that
house in between the smoking but some of its people are still living]

'I want you to leave your body now' he tells me

his voice not so much hypnotic as reaching
for the hypnotic

but I leave it anyway sitting in the upright chair
of the windowless room

for a place higher up that's not quite
the windowless room –

though I'm aware of my body's particular kind
of breathing down there

dressed in my favourite shirt and somehow
up here I'm dressed

in that same shirt which is I feel suddenly
becoming very important

its colour pertaining to a quiet hue of knowing
I can't quite explain

and I do not think about the money I have
given him   the man who is speaking

but I'm looking instead down on a yellow
kitchen in Swindon

upon a tiny remembered body I have found
crying or about to cry

in little white shorts and there is carpet
streaked with blue

and there is the noise of a terrible thing
that is happening

and there is summer outside with its
other children

'he doesn't understand does he'
says the man

'he is so young' and I understand the shirt
that he will have to grow through

all of the terrible things to fit
I can feel my body now

filling up the space inside its soft and
lavender-scented cotton

whenI

firstbe

ganto

speakp

ublicly

aboutm

ydysfunctional

family

mymoth

er~~was~~

~~enraged~~

~~toherm~~

~~yachiev~~

~~ementswereas~~

~~ignthat~~

~~Icouldnothavesuffered~~

~~'thatmuch'inournuclearf~~

~~amilyye~~

~~tIknowIsurvivedand~~thri

ved~~des~~

~~pitethepaino~~

~~fchild~~

~~hood~~

here's your mother she is Patti Smith and gazes hungry

in November   in 1969   in Manhattan in the Horn and Hardart automat

    upon a sandwich   in a vending machine   behind its glass

    with one less dime in her hand than she needs

just then your dad appears dressed as Allen Ginsberg

buys her the sandwich and now she has to sit

and listen to him talk   about Walt Whitman

    for the rest of her life

but instead of talking about Walt Whitman

he is silent   suddenly they are both rotated 90 degrees to the left

    and instead of an automat

    there are only armchairs a carpeted living room a TV

[in the dream...his father was alive once more and was talking to him in his usual way but the remarkable thing was that he was nevertheless dead only did not know it] one story goes a man on his lunch break was hit

   by a falling baby falling from a very high window

of a building the man was passing on his lunch break

the man saved the baby's life accidentally getting landed on

   the man saved that exact baby's life accidentally getting landed on

one exact year later   on his lunch break breaking

the slightly-more-grown-baby-falling-

from-the-same-window's fall accidentally

the man's name is   Joseph Figlock what is sad is

the realisation this baby

could literally mean anything

but doesn't

it does not

what I don't know is whether that baby

a toddler by now   has fallen a third time

whether he is falling still and at this moment crying out

where is Joseph Figlock I can't see him why isn't he here

elsewhere a man is cutting down a tree
he works at it night and day his big heaving chest
grown tired sawing at that thick trunk
after a long while the tree is still standing though
at a tilt towards his house where his family sit
there is a pie in the oven
there are toys and the laughter of children
it is a beautiful home
but he's come this far and it's taken so much effort

[the 'he' could refer to either the father or the son in other words the son could be dead and not know it]

when he is dancing in a red field at nighttime
he is not dancing in a red field at nighttime   but standing there thinks
I am now
the sort of person who dances   in a red field at nighttime: that's me
while everybody else is just dancing
truth be told I've never danced
    in an anything at nighttime
        or cried much   or hugged my mother
            or swam in lakes in the middle of woodlands
on the outskirts of Berlin
            in a place called Krumme Lanke   with my daughter
and my girlfriend
I dip my toes in that's all   and think
    I'm now the sort of person who swims in
        lakes in the middle of woodlands
            on the outskirts of Berlin
                in a place called Krumme Lanke
and who knows he doesn't really and has things very wrong with him
astronomical-unfair things that preclude me
like death   somewhere tucked under the armpit   the thought of it
    and a tangerine ache somewhere in my wrist
        that feels disgusting and I could be dead
soon or someone else could
        a scratching so far into my chest there is no more skin
my girlfriend is watching me be all these things beside our picnic
and my daughter is
smiling my feet wet there in all these thoughts

'the soul is what grows on things when they last' said a man
who didn't have any problems

    Dear Anything please   let me last across this moment
and on just a bit more
my body is busy thinking itself unwell   my body is
thinking itself outside of this moment
what if the soul this moment is cultivating is just an unwell thought I'm piling
on top all of the other very disturbing thoughts   until they stand up inside me
someone I love dying from me thinking or not thinking
    about the very specific circumstances of it
        fear of very specific types of bacteria   and cancer of the mouth lung
the brain very specifically haemorrhaging all the harm I could do
what I do is I take these and I keep them safe inside me
I have to organise them have to keep them
very tidy   each little shit thing
        what I have to do is count through each one
what if my body fell away and this soul I'm building was just a thing
        left sweating alone in the finicky sun
    I'm laughing my whole self into my sad sleeve
    at what this has so quickly become but wait:
I can come back from this
            everybody loves a comeback so I'm calling myself back
            backwards into the lake   it can happen
green shadows are all over the place at once   here goes
            the sun is suggesting I get over myself
    and my daughter is laughing   I look silly doing it here goes
        the water is very calm everyone is dancing the rhythm is in me

let's get down to the boiled
beef of it let's get down to
the canned ham the corned
beef hash of it the pickled
herring the rump steak let's
get right down and inside the
black pudding the shepherd's
pie of this stuff let's tuck
right into the sausage and
mash the battered cod of it
the jar of mussels the pork
loin tender loin the liver and
onions of the thing let's dig
deep into the chicken and
chips the turkey thigh of
this business the sizzling
bacon the eggs of it *no foreign
muck* lamb shank gammon
you've got a screw loose my
father's face fastening and
unfastening around mouthfuls
of pheasant the game

[rip open my right lung and probably you'll find cig
ash butts a staunch inability to leave my dad behind
and something like a dirty great cow
getting roasted in all the heat]

here's your mother she is Demi Moore

with short black hair

it's the early nineties she's not got much on

    sitting at her pottery wheel

The Righteous Brothers are singing about love

it might be raining outside and dark

    and she's getting pretty messy there in all that clay

you might think   you might expect at this moment

the well-toned the shirtless husband

to arrive behind her in tight black jeans

    but nothing

only the record spinning and the empty symbol

of the half-finished jar lengthening on that wheel

what is sad is there is even an intimacy
to getting mugged David
a confined planet in which the emptiness in you is landed on
by another person two persons watching perhaps more
and for a minute your body is very much the focus of something
persons – you are one of them – very close in the dark
taking up – for a moment – less space
senses open and full of corrosive love
enter canned laughter here
enter a fist or forehead is crashing through my living now
     and all over my buttoned-down shirt
ask me my favourite word: alive
and thinking of all the ways out of this sitcom I'm in
and laughter
not a type that is with you not a type
you know in the centre of your eardrum to be at you
but the type of laughter you're not certain is there   that you have
to check and strain and check leaning over and over
the barrel a barrel of laughs you can't get out of

[I stuff my empty stomach full of smoke
the same way in a back alley a lady
stuffs
a kitten
into
a
dustbin]

keep the friends keep the imminent
laughter vacuum-packed like meat
served up comfy as comfy as apple
sauce in the mouth keep this guy
ubiquitous as straight teeth dancing
in posh black shoes no tie keep the
clean white streak of his girlfriend's
quirk dancing in posh black shoes
dancing in posh black shoes the
other almost-swappable four keep
the incoming canned laughter comfy
as applesauce it's so funny to be
normal so hard to imagine an illness
in your head going off loud like a
fake studio audience when there's a
sofa this happy music opening
shutting half-hugs it's hard to
visualise my body dying unless it's
followed by the unreal lip-smacking
laughter these scenes are followed
by here I've been followed by that
lip-smacking laughter down every
street switched lights on and off in
every room of the house to make
certain of something been fat and
thin clapped my hands onetwothree
four the hunger inside me is a
fountain recycling its own water

somewhere in Florida a snake is overwhelming itself with the dead cow it has found in an everglade with absolutely no regard for the impact on its own physique it is walking its unfused jaws all over the thing digesting before it has even finished eating those salivary glands are working like a motherfucker that spine and body the snake is crawling through its food on the long journey toward a place it likes to sleep what is sad is how many people are having sex like this and calling it something else let the snake keep the dead cow it maybe deserves maybe does not what's important is somewhere one of the things you think you don't deserve is happening to someone else while you are unpacking all your failed relationships into a small glass jar

what is sad is I wrote your name all over my jeans
keep the jeans keep the three-meat sandwich we ate
the rap song we made up together in a bedroom
at your house then mine with our parents getting
drunk downstairs and despising each other keep the
elderly woman we both wanted to be on her bike
riding her bike no hands keep the elderly woman
we saw cold and knocked down in the street circled
by an ambulance and an ambulance everything
zooming out and away from her keep the touching
when we touched our boy bodies in out-of-the-way
places in places that were out of the way keep those
David keep your alcoholic mum who left her family
to live on the streets keep the children who hate her
now the husband who did the washing up but also
slapped her in the face sometimes I'm sorry nothing
changed keep the woman throw away the husband
keep my own scar on my upper lip the weight loss
meat-based   accelerating into the future

[canned laughter]

I'm shitting butterflies out from my granulated stomach
and back into the world getting smaller
and smaller the man in the windowless room I can hear
his long-suffering wife shuffle on the cream-carpeted
landing on the street that used to be my street I'm
thinking of the two French women with vigorous
haircuts they are still bicycle thieves rapaciously pumping
up the worn down tyres of an old blue chopper
the nervous nervous customer a blond man biting his nails
is checking his phone wondering how long
can this possibly go on for
can't entirely get the fuck out of my body today
in the windowless room the man is telling me to stop
writing things down like a victim and be more like a warrior

[I once had a dream that at his funeral my father suddenly sat
bolt upright in his coffin and asked 'did you hear
the one about…?']

did you hear the one about the two teenaged boys
who loved each other by not eating
one would occasionally watch the other vomit
into the bathroom sink the other would wipe
the back of his pin-striped sleeve around the bowels of bone-
grey porcelain and ask forgiveness for cheating
which one of us was David kicking a football so hard
into a crowd of drunk dads or through the window
of the dirty butcher with his hairless legs beneath an apron
our mums buying us secret cans of strawberry slimfast for school
lunchtimes they were so supportive dinnertimes there were stacks
of pizza slices piled up next to the neighbourhood dogs
and o there was a girl
at the end of the street we both saw ourselves properly lost to
my god she was skinny a higher volley
of abandon than our bodies might ever hope to reach

[*canned laughter*]

what is sad
is the unknown
of her back
is so much of your eyes close-up
on her body and writhing
a strange basilica is her breast bone
is a naked cup of cold milk   is the choral groan
in her throat her finger raised is agreeing hard
in this light all of this love is yours
is your surging wish
to die is that you would sing out loud for this person
is that your voice is in your throat
your heart is in your chest
your mind in your head
your eyes are there in their sockets
in your body
on this chair
in this room further back and darker
than you ever thought possible

sadthedirtygreatbovinedaydoesnotsing

untilthepainforksthemiddleo

f

i

t

s

h

o

o

v

e

s

if you piled each of my bad thoughts on top of the next
eventually they would be the size of the tallest cow in the world
his name is Daniel
he lives in a field in America
the previous tallest cow on earth they say was of such volume
it cracked its hind legs and had
to be put down this is the closest to suicide a cow can get – eating too much
some humans eat cows some mimic them
Daniel's owner is constantly checking the news
for updates on cow size
and when he is not he is out in the fields with a measuring tape

I'm ridding my body of itself
moving backwards from the milk
gradually unlearning how to make cottage pie
when I die
bury me in the nimbus over a cattle shed

DAD'S DICK

FLOPPY DOG TONGUE

PIG'S SNOUT

CHIP SHOP SAUSAGE ON SATURDAY AFTERNOONS

LYRIC I OF SUNDAY LUNCHES

MEAT PROTAGONIST

CENTRE OF ALL NARRATIVE DÉNOUEMENT

NEVER READ A BOOK NEVER COOKED YOURSELF

A MEAL

SWITCH ON THE OVEN

O ORGANISER OF THE FAMILY UNIT

AVID KEEPER OF NUMBERS

YOU'RE FULL TO THE BRIM WITH FLINCHING

TO THE BRIM WITH NOTHING

VIOLENCE

LIFTER OF TOILET SEATS

MAKER OF STAINS

ITCHER

NERVOUS TWITCHER

DRUNKARD

STITCHER UP OF MOTHERS

REST EASY YOUR WORK HERE IS DONE

o anxiety keep the secret it returns

often and like fear of bus rides like canned laughter

or babies crying arrives again like a school bully or the wide sleep

of dead dads

and since it happens from the outside–in

    you think maybe it can be avoided for a bit like mayonnaise

can look around for proof it's just some egg-like joke   and yet

it's everywhere like magic like mods in the 60s Christian rock stars in Tennessee

like unemployment   smashed schoolboys

it's under the bun in the salad on the corners of the mouths

of the people you love

a bit on the light switch door handles some on the carpet

the taste of it replicating itself like a pop song's chorus

on the tongue of the man down the road of the women in pubs

all humming between cigarette puffs and learning its words

starlings in Arkansas

like turtle doves hung on trees
like the second day of Christmas
blackbirds abandoning themselves pretty much everywhere
keep these birds the sky is chucking them out of its mouth
in 2011 the cats getting fat off these bodies
tearing the sparkle from their getting-pink bodies
belching and coughing out inked-up quills
all the dads probably shaking their heads over coffee
probably slamming their mugs down too hard
before stepping out to work keep the work
what is sad is the women in corduroy and plaid
rubbing the cats' cabbage-patch tummies
packing the kids off to school
then collecting the hairless corpses of birds
lining them up naked like letters of rejection
in neat rows on the carpet

Sundays he cuts first his Yorkshire pudding I cut first my Yorkshire pudding she stands in the kitchen smoking later he will say an unkind thing the whole of the world is arranged around our television set later I will step over his drunkwhite and outofwork body

Sundays she stands in the kitchen tenderising a cow the cow of course is dead and wrapped up in cling film he stopped years ago cleaning his teeth years ago he put his toothbrush away and turned his back on the bathroom sink for good

I cut first my Yorkshire pudding she wears her endless wedding ring removes her wedding ring to do the washing up alone later he will say an unkind thing I will step overhisdrunk whiteand out of work body

the cow of course is dead the cow is covered in gravy now there are also peas Sundays there was a tooth on his pillow which he hid he hid it the whole of the world is arranged around that tooth now in hiding or the gaps in his mouth later she will do the washing up

take off her ring later he will say an unkind thing there are also peas the television set is speaking to the room the room is silent I cut first my Yorkshire pudding again I am zipped up and frantic with fear the cow of course is dead honey glazed potatoes

the protection of a cup final kids' match on Sunday
ruined by a football smashed against a crossbar
my team mates their parents
all despoiling in the sad horrible sun

my dad
I'm sorry I suddenly turned on him
and chinned the fucker

[I flung open a random drawer
in the room
   next to the one
     in which he died
and there I found a small ring box
   full of my own milk teeth]

fall – I'm taking chequered carpets
and panelled bathrooms with me
taking the whole damn house
I'm running on thin air   half your short head of hair
bits of you coming away between my fingers
27 years ago was perfect clawing toward you David
feeling the weight too much around our ribs now I don't
I'm riding myself backwards when the moon is bright
you can make your body a palindrome
I can always see you lit in the window of your parents' bedroom
my only friend and measuring yourself nakeder than me
my only friend hating bits of his body that aren't there jeez
there we are like a drawn-out TV show
call it N-E-V-E-R T-H-I-N E-N-O-U-G-H
call it one thousand saccharine emotions soused in Marlboro Light
yes the wallpaper is blue because I am depressed
we are so bad for each other always
you could be a plumber by now and muscly
and I am barely here remembering how great it all felt [*canned laughter*]
before I said out loud I just wanted someone beautiful
to sit down validate me and listen
as the foxes instead of stealing from the kitchens of east London
are fucking wailing into the 5 and 6 ams

in the morning all of her pain

is trying to happen at the top of its voice

drivers shutting off engines at the bus stop

hanging out their cracked-open doors blue jackets

this woman too old to be my mother or she's not

too dressed in a felt hat & cashmere or she isn't

traffic is backing up along the road now

a small then big crowd making itself up around her body

and she is reaching her fingers right down inside herself

to pull it all up for everyone to see

a botched magic trick

flowers stuck inside her throat

there are things like this I'm worried I can't stop

a static black cab's engine like a drumroll

absolute sadness I cannot prevent

an enormous wrench and she comes up empty   nothing

but her palms are on her knees and she's slow   dry-heaving

this woman does not have my mother's mouth or she does

all of her pain is trying to happen at the top of its voice

a botched magic trick

meanwhile rabbits growing out the eyes of a child

and the woman holding its hand   fistfuls of rabbits

white and black fur bloating in everyone

your dad randy and playful
slapping your half-cut mum's
bum on the sofa
the one cherished thing
you are able to hold in the bin of childhood
with the lid up for as long as possible
slamming it shut just before
his clumsiness the both of them
your mother a little too hard laughing off the awkwardness of her
middle finger
snapped

butthemothermustbenobleandheragonyredemptive

withthesufferingofthewholeworldetchedonherface

the posh mums are boxing in the square

roughing each other up   in a nice way

this is not the world into which I was born

       so I'm changing it

I'm sinking deep into the past and dressing my own mum

in their blue spandexes

svelte black stripes from hip to hem

and husbands with better dispositions toward kindness

or at least   I'm giving her new lungs

I'm giving her a best friend   with no problems and both of them pads

some gloves to go at each other with   in a nice way

I'm making it a warm day for them but also

I'm making it rain

the two of them dapping it out in long shadows

I'm watching her from the trees grow

strength in her thighs   my mum

grow strength in her glutes my mum

her back taut upright

her knees

and watching her grow no bad thing in her stomach no tumour

her feet do not hurt to touch   my mum she is hopping

sinews are happening

wiry arms developing their full reach

no bad thing explodes

sweat and not gradual death   I'm cheering

no thing in her stomach no alcohol

no cigarettes with their crotonaldehyde let my dad keep those

no removal of her womb

– and I'm cheering her on in better condition

cheering she is learning to fight for her own body
in spandex her new life
and though there is no beef between them
if her friend is gaining the upper hand
I will call out from the trees
          her name
                    Christine!
and when she turns   as turn she must
my mum   in the nicest possible way
can slug her right in the gut

[it was so clearly the end of a movie when she smiled
and though I don't want anything to end I do want what she had
then a sense of victory a nougaty climax a little tasty]

BALL BOY

IF YOU

SQUINT

HARD AS IT GOES IN

THROUGH THE PAINTED WHITE

OF ITS FRAMEWORK

FOR THE FIFTH TIME

YOU'LL SEE A TINY VERSION OF ME

TRACKSUITED

AND WADDLING

UP FROM THE BACK OF THE NET

TO KICK

THE THING BACK OUT AGAIN

[as if a sign from the kismet
the man arrives outside my window
with his breathing in an old person's shopping trolley
his lungs two defunct pieces of steak
and possibly a bladder infection
ask me my favourite word: alive]

into the 5 and 6 ams
I keep having this same dream
my tongue is too big for my mouth
a numb slab of carpaccio a slew fish pounded thin
my body froze – it takes an enormous affect
a throwing forward of the soul to make it go anywhere
a man twists the shirt collar hard beneath a woman's chin
a kid gets his pockets patted down
by five other kids and just stands there
beneath a clean window
my daughter with her knees
to her chest is growing
and I'm starting to get
death's cruel joke setting itself up around my eyes
its punchline I'm accelerating into
so early so early

look-see: I am going to meet him

in the middle

in the middle

we are going to hit – we are

hitting pause

on this whole thing

then hitting

a little two-step number

biting thickly on each other's necks

don'tleaveth

eroomuntil

Icomebac

kfromt

hedea

dfor

yo

u

finally we find out how he died   the house burned
while he was rescuing the kids the dog the photo album all
the emotional music and you are crying the cat beside you
and our hands not holding hands but very close to doing it
he didn't it turns out die inside that house
but miles down the road with bits of it still on fire inside him
please god thank you
we've gotten to valentine's day again quick maths
skidding past us like trees

    you have two more tattoos

    I have three more spots at my hairline

    you have a porn account now

    and one new dance move

    and I have a dirty great sum totting itself up

    above my head – a smoke alarm

    the switch on our crock pot is not faulty

    the pilot lights on all the household

    appliances are working fine

survive

andifyoumakeamistakeyougetpunishedforitbut

that'sno

bigthing

yoube

come

strong

doing

theth

ingsy

ounee

dtobe

stron

gfor

NOTES

Page 9: Franz Kafka, *Letter to His Father*

Page 21: bell hooks, *All About Love: New Visions*

Page 23, 26 & 37: Danae Clark, 'Father Figure', *BOYS: Masculinity in Contemporary Culture*

Page 40 is reworking of a phrase from one of the Buddha's discourses, via Jean Valentine

Page 52 & 53: Jacqueline Rose, *Mothers: An Essay on Love and Cruelty*

Page 60 (lines 10-17): Richard Siken, 'You Are Jeff', *Crush*

Page 62: Audre Lorde, 'A Conversation with Adrienne Rich', *Your Silence Will Not Protect You*